Freelancing

I0470401

Making Money Online With Freelancing Jobs

Written By Robert Kempster

Table of Contents

Introduction

Welcome to my instructional freelancing book. Numerous times, I have been asked to create a book to help people start out in the freelancing industry, and I have finally made the time to get this book written. It was freelancers who had struggled or are struggling that came to me and asked me to write this book, so I took their suggestions seriously. This book is a guide to starting out in the freelancing trade. If you're already freelancing successfully, then you may not find it as useful, but remember that there is always something new to be learned, and knowledge is priceless.

Freelancing can be an enjoyable job if you do it the right way. Do it the wrong way, and it can be a stressful and emotional time. The key to success in anything is planning, and freelancing isn't any different from any other task that you decide to take on. You can't just wake up one day and expect to make a fortune. Nothing ever comes that easy, but with hard work, the right attitude, and proper advice, you will make it in the freelancing world.

Inside this book, I will cover every step that you need to take to set yourself up for a successful career freelancing. From choosing the right service to provide that suits your talents and skills, to branding both yourself and your business services, using freelancer sites to get established, branching out and building your own websites, clients and other useful information that every freelancer should be aware of.

There is usually a reason that people choose to take on freelancing as a profession. Some people may be looking to enjoy a healthier and happier home/life balance. Freelancing gives them the opportunity to spend time at home with their family. For other people, they may be looking to earn extra income to supplement their day job. In tough economic times, we all do what we have to do to support ourselves and our families. Freelancing can be the perfect way to use your skills to generate an extra income stream, and over time it could become your primary source of revenue. For others, they may have lost their regular job, and freelancing could be the only way they have to support themselves and earn an income.

Freelancing, like most things, will require you to start at the bottom of the pile and work your way up to the top. Depending on skills you have and what service you are looking to provide, it could happen quicker for you or slower. The important thing to remember is to take your time and make sure that you do a good job. Establishing yourself and earning a good reputation will be what eventually helps you make more money and start getting yourself some great regular clients.

In this day and age, your online reputation is extremely important. Online reviews of products, businesses, and services are growing at a rapid pace, along with the online commerce world. Consumers, whether they are buying your services or products, are looking at your reviews and ratings and doing their homework before they buy.

This doesn't mean that you have to work for nothing, but initially you may need to price yourself according to your online reputation and client base, not your skill level. Once you have a good reputation and work is starting to flow your way, then you can look at increasing prices, or branching out into other services.

Freelancing can be the perfect way to make an income without having to travel to work, find childcare services, or deal with employers. You can make your own hours, and choose which jobs you decide to take on and which jobs you decline. The great thing about freelancing is in most cases you can take your workplace with you wherever you go, anywhere in the world. For most freelancers, all they need is their laptop and an Internet connection to get their work done. You don't even need the greatest Internet connection. As long as you can check in with clients, get your work done, you don't need to be online 24/7.

Once you make it as a successful freelancer, you can decide for yourself if it's the right time to move into freelancing full time. You need to evaluate for yourself how you think your work is going to continue if it will be consistent and if you will make enough money to support yourself between jobs. Never rely on one good client to support you. You should always be looking for new customers, but don't over commit yourself either. Communication is key when you're freelancing or in any other job you take on. If everyone is on the same page about deadlines, then they will be happier knowing what is going on and more understanding if you need more time to finish a task.

If you are already freelancing, then you may have advanced past what this book could offer you in most cases, but remember even one great piece of advice could be the diamond among the rough. It could be the one new thing that you learn from this book that takes your business to the next level, creating the lifestyle that you have only ever dreamed of!

Chapter One: Choosing the Right Service to Provide

These days, almost every service can be outsourced. Businesses are learning that they don't need to employ someone to sit in an office to answer phones or a web designer to work on their website. Now they can just hire someone on a project-based rate. When they're not needed, then they don't need to pay them. This is true even for something traditional such as receptionists who answer your calls. You can setup anyone anywhere in the world to answer your phones, take messages, make appointments, and manage the general day-to-day operations of your business. The Internet and technology are opening up a lot of opportunities for people to step in and make a good living, all from the comfort of their own homes, or anywhere in the world. You could be relaxing on a tropical island, and still be making some significant money while you drink cocktails and soak up some sunshine.

You will need to get yourself setup to start freelancing, but this doesn't have to be expensive. These days, you can purchase yourself a reliable laptop for anywhere from $300-$1,000 depending on how much money you are looking to spend. If you have a laptop or computer, then you are halfway there already. Just make sure that it's reliable. Another thing to consider when you're trying to decide between a laptop and a regular desktop computer is whether or not you'll be travelling. A laptop is a lot more convenient if you plan on working away from home, and even if you plan on moving around inside your home. You'll also need to make sure that you have a reliable Internet connection. A decent home connection is perfect, and you can even get a mobile internet USB stick so that you can take your Internet with you if you're travelling. You may need to purchase some new software programs so that you're up to date with the latest editions. Don't rush out and buy everything to begin with, just purchase what you need to have initially. Setup a PayPal account or bank account and you're ready to get started!

So now that you are prepared to step into the exciting world of freelancing, you have some things that you'll need to work out. When you set out down the path of freelancing, the very first thing that you'll need to establish is what service you are going to provide. You have to be realistic here, and consider that there are already a lot of people doing this, so don't expect to get jobs as a graphic design artist or engineer unless you actually are one. If you are qualified and competent in whatever area you choose to focus on, then you will soon start getting clients and moving towards the next steps of your freelancing career.

Just because you don't have skills such as a website designer or publisher, it won't eliminate you from becoming a freelancer. You may have other secondary skills such as typing, answering phone calls, data entry, etc. The list of skills that people are looking for is endless. You don't have to be able to do everything that an office administrator does to be able to succeed as a freelancer. That's the great thing about it. People are looking for a variety of different freelancers who can do various aspects of the work they want. Sure, some people will be looking for someone who is qualified to do everything, but you will soon find out that you can carve out a niche market of work for yourself.

Popular Freelancing Services

Here is a list of some of the most common freelancing services that people are supplying:

Marketing – This can be broken down into a lot of smaller categories. Marketing Coordinator, Project Manager, Marketing Assistant, Marketing Manager, and Research Assistant.

Business Project Management – There are several smaller branches to business management. Project Manager, Project Analyst, and Project Manager's Assistant.

Web Development – This has several branches that you can choose from. Web Application Developer, Junior Developer, Web Content Developer, and Web Development Manager.

Writing – With a little skill and creativity, you can definitely get a great start in writing. Content Manager, Ghost Writing, Web Content Writing, Editor, Technical Writing, Blog & Article Writing, or Proofreading and Review Writing.

Accounting – If you have any skills with numbers, this could be for you. Accounting Clerk, Property Accountant, Accountant, Bookkeeper, and Financial Consultant.

Tutoring & Teaching – There is the world full of people looking for language instructions. Teacher, Tutor, Language Tutor, Teacher's Assistant, and Research Assistant.

Social Media – This is a broad group. Pinterest, Facebook, Twitter, Email Campaigns and management, Advertising, Forum Management, and Website Management.

Graphic Design – Digital Designer, Visual Designer, Graphic Design Assistant, Communications Designer, Website Design, and Graphic Artist.

Administrative Assistance – Here is a good place for beginners to start in the freelancing industry. Executive Assistant, Personal Assistant, Virtual Assistant, and Administrative Assistant.

Even if you only have core competencies in any of these fields, then you should be able to work yourself in at an entry level. Start by picking a general area, and then work out what you can and can't do. There are also a lot of courses available online or at community or technical colleges that will help get your skill levels up.

When you're applying for positions as a freelancer, people will be less interested in seeing a resume as such, and more interested in seeing results. If you do a small job to prove that you are capable, then that in most cases will be enough to secure you a starting position. Remember, good results, and prompt, clear communication are among the most desirable traits that employees are looking for in freelancers. They want to know what you're doing, when you will be finished, and that you understand what they require from you.

Just be sure to do your research before you start out freelancing. Common sense is the golden rule when considering any business opportunity, no matter what it is. The world is full of people who are looking to take advantage of others. Remember, if it sounds too good to be true, then it most likely is. Do your homework, read online reviews, and in most cases you don't need to hand over any money to start on freelancing sites.

Chapter Two: Branding Yourself and Your Services

Once you have decided which service you are going to provide, it is time to start to build up your online reputation. Before you can just get yourself a website and have clients looking for you, you'll need to build up your reputation and brand. Freelancing can be an excellent way to build client lists and have a base income coming in before you branch out on your own. You may earn less than usual freelancing initially, but the benefits in the end could be well worth the reduced rate in the beginning. Consider this as a promotional discount on your brand, much like you would have a discount on a product you were considering releasing.

Freelancing online is not the same as applying for jobs in your everyday life. Potential employers are less interested in what you have done earlier in your career and more interested in what you can do for them and their business. In theory, you could have been fired from several jobs or have an adverse recommendation from an employer, and they won't care. Potential clients are more interested in getting an excellent product at a good price; actions speak a lot louder than words in the freelancing world. When you start freelancing online, it is in essence a new beginning, but this doesn't mean that you can afford to throw away opportunities.

There are a lot of different freelancing platforms available online for you to choose from. Many have similar formats, and some may require you to pay a small fee for you to be able to bid on jobs that become available. Others require you to pay to boost your applications, and the rest are entirely free. What I recommend is that you choose several of the freelancing sites, build your profile, and then drop them as you see results or not. This way you will have several different options on the go, and you can easily work on more than one platform at once. If a site requires little attention, and you only receive one or two good jobs, then it doesn't cost you much to keep that site active to attract potential clients. You never know when the next small client turns into that great client that keeps you busy for years down the track.

The first thing that you will need to do is login and create an account and user profile. Many sites will allow you to upload a video to your profile, and this is always recommended to boost potential views of your profile. You will need to link your profile to a payment method also, such as a bank account, or PayPal account, and some sites will require this name to match so remember that also. When you create your profile, choose a real picture of yourself to make your profile seem as realistic as possible. The more people feel as if you are a real person, the more they will be able to feel comfortable interacting with you.

Now that you have your profile created, and you have setup your account, it's time to move onto the next stage. Before you start applying for jobs and projects, there will be in most cases tests that you can do to prove that you have some core competencies in whatever field you have chosen as your service. These tests will either be free, or you may have to pay a small fee for every test that you wish to take. They range from basic English language skills, email skills, social media tests, all the way through to programming and graphic design work. Showing that you are already somewhat qualified can be a big advantage when you're applying for jobs. If the tests are free, then I recommend doing as many as possible if you are experienced in them. Building up your profile as much as possible will help you not only when applying for potential jobs, but also when clients are looking for freelancers.

The way freelancing sites will vary from site to site, no two are exactly the same, but all are similar enough that you should be able to create a profile and find your way around. Getting those first few projects will always be the hardest obstacle to overcome. Once you have completed some jobs and received good feedback from clients, every job after that will become easier to land.

The way freelancing sites work is similar in most cases; the fundamental idea is that you create a profile and either search for work on the site or let employers find you.

Let's take Fiverr for example. The basic idea behind Fiverr is that your gig or job is five dollars. You can then add extras on to build up your position to the amount you want. It's an excellent platform to get started on, as it will cost you nothing to set up and start working. Fiverr is a lot more buyer proactive than other freelancing sites. Customers are more likely to come to you looking for your services, but there is also a small buyer request area that is updated daily that freelancers can apply to. Having a good profile and feedback will make your profile more likely to pop up for potential clients.

When you go to a freelancing sites such as Upwork (which is a merger between oDesk and Elance), clients will post their projects and it is up to you to apply for these positions. Same thing here with your feedback and profile, the more complete it is, the more attractive your proposal will be to potential clients. With most freelancing sites, there will be a daily, weekly, or monthly limit to how many positions that you can apply for. This is to prevent people applying for every position and ruining the system with bad applications. Some freelancing sites may make you pay a small amount to apply for jobs, or they may make you pay if you want to go over your limit.

It's strongly suggested that in the beginning you offer services as cheaply as possible until you start to either build up a list of clients or get yourself some good feedback. There will always be plenty of people looking for the cheapest work possible in the quickest turnaround time in exchange for good feedback. Once you get some work coming in, and you begin to have clients coming to you, then you can start to choose what work you want, and what you will charge. Some clients are happy to pay more once they have formed a relationship with a good freelancer; others will move on to the next cheapest freelancer that they can find. Try not to consider your lower prices as a big loss too much at the beginning. Instead, consider this as promotional work to build your brand and profile on the freelancing platform.

There are a lot of different freelancing platforms available online, I'm not going to list every single one out there, but I will list a top 25 freelancing sites for you to get a start on. Remember before you hand over any money for anything, if it sounds too good to be true, then it very well could be. Take your time, and do your homework on the freelancing sites, read the reviews online, and consider them before you invest any money into them.

Trusted and Popular List of 25 Freelancing Sites

These first sites are freelance sites more suited for content writers, data entry operators, website designers, developers, programmers, and graphic artists. These freelancing sites will also offer plenty of opportunity for virtual assistants and any other online job position available.

www.freelancer.com

www.upwork.com

www.guru.com

www.jobs.problogger.net/

www.craiglist.com

www.ifreelance.com

www.peopleperhour.com

www.gofreelance.com

www.demandstudios.com

www.project4hire.com

www.fiverr.com

www.allfreelancework.com

www.online-writing-jobs.com/

www.freelancewritinggigs.com

www.journalismjobs.com   *This is great for people interested in journalism.*

The next job sites are more tailored towards programmers, web designers, and logo or banner creators.

www.toptal.com

www.rent-acoder.com

www.getacoder.com

www.99designs.com

www.scriptlance.com

www.logomyway.com

www.programmermeetdesigner.com

www.projectspring.com

www.eprojects.co.in

www.ejobs4pros.com

Remember to build up your profile as quickly as possible. Take those cheaper jobs to get some projects and feedback on your profile, and then start to look into the more profitable jobs available. Once you get your profile to a certain level, you won't even have to apply for work anymore, employers will come looking for you!

I have a ton more information I'd like to share with you which you can get simply by following this link: MORE INFORMATION or by going to https://mailchi.mp/1a871d9a8fe3/landingpage

No spam, I promise!

Chapter Three: Branding Yourself and Your Services

Now that you have created your freelancing profile, and you have started working or looking for work, it is time to think about the future. What are you looking to get out of your freelancing career? Most sites control how much you can make, how you operate on their sites, and they charge fees or a commission on everything you earn or spend. If you are happy to go along paying their fees and being limited to what you can do, then just continue the way you are. If you have any interest in branching out and getting away from someone else controlling how you work, then it is time to think about your branding.

Be aware that it is in these freelancing sites' best interest to keep you using their platforms. They don't want you to work offsite; they want to keep getting a commission of your sales. It is against their terms of service to take work off-site, and some sites don't even allow you to communicate with buyers off of the platform. If you start telling all of your clients just to work through your website, then you may find yourself being banned or having your account suspended.

There are hundreds of millions of freelancers working online at any one time. They may come and go quickly, but there will always be a core group of freelancers who you are directly competing against.

Remember, there is always someone else working who will get the job done quicker and cheaper than you, so getting your list of clients and creating a brand for yourself is incredibly important. How will you get people to start looking for you, and coming to you for their work?

Branding Yourself and Your Services is The Answer!

Your success working as a freelancer will be determined by how memorable you can make yourself. You want your clients to have you listed as their go-to freelancer. When you have repeat customers coming to you, willing to wait for your services, and pay a premium, then you know that you are doing something right. Creating your brand and getting yourself to this position isn't impossible, it isn't even that hard, all it will take is a little bit of your time and effort. This investment of time and work will pay for itself well and truly in a return of labor and some great clients.

There are two different ways that we can approach the problem of branding yourself and your services as a freelancer.

- *You can create a business name that will let everyone know what service you provide, or*
- *Use your name, but come up with a catchphrase that will stick with people and allow them to remember you and your service.*

Freelancers can have good results using either approach, so ultimately it will be up to you which one you choose to implement.

They will both get some great results, so think about it before you start down either direction, you don't want to have to go over it again if you change your mind.

Your ultimate goal when you decide to start branding yourself is to put a consistent image or brand out there, and remain consistent across all your work. You want your brand to be consistent across your freelancing, your website, business cards, social media, and anything other where your brand comes into play. Following these simple steps and remaining consistent will help you create your brand, and keep your images and branding consistent across the field.

Develop Your Own Unique Selling Proposition or USP

Don't rush into any of this. Take your time, and do your research before you just buy any website URL that is available. Think about what it is that defines you as a freelancer in the first place, is it what you work on, what you produce, or how you produce your work? It doesn't matter what you decide these are; your brand needs to reflect on your ideas of what makes you unique. You need to think about what it is you are going to offer, and how people will be looking for your services.

If you provide more than one service, pick which one you are going to focus on, and then this will need to be reflected in your branding. There aren't a lot of points trying to brand yourself as a "freelance writer, photographer, website builder, and graphic design artist."

It's just too much going on, and you will only get a small return on each, instead of a real return on one. You can still provide all of these services, but for your branding, try to stick to one or two at most.

Do Your Homework on Your Business Brand Name

Now that you have determined which service you are going to focus on, then it is time to start thinking about whether or not you're going with the catchy business name or using your name as your branding.

This is where it will pay to do some research before you commit to anything. Do some research online, check your keywords, and see what else is out there online. Check available website addresses and prices to obtain them. Some are quite expensive, while other will turn out to be less popular but more affordable.

It is Time to Choose the Appropriate URL For You

Your name as your URL will always be the cheaper option to begin with, unless your name happens to be the same as a famous movie star, in which case you could be in trouble! Your branding business name will be more expensive, depending on what services you are offering as a freelancer. Whichever way you go, it's a good idea to buy your name either way. This way you have locked it down for later if you become famous! You never know when it could become useful to you in the future.

When you choose your URL try to get some great search words into your URL. Try to think about what people will write when they are searching, what words they will combine, or what services will most commonly be referred to. You always need to think about how people will write when they are searching, not just what services you offer as a freelancer.

Remember to keep your branding consistent here. Use the same keywords as you have in your URL across your website and social media campaigns.

Choose Yourself a Catchy Tagline

Try to keep your tagline as short as possible. A full paragraph isn't going to work. Keep it simple and to the point so that people will be able to not only remember it, but it will be more likely to pop up when they search for it.

Now it is Time to Think About Integrating Your Brand into the Website Design

Remember that branding isn't just the words that you choose as your tagline or the way you describe yourself or your services. Your branding has to include not only words but also images and your style. When you are creating your website, remember that if you have a particular color, style, logo, or image, then continue that through your website's theme and any email correspondence or when you deliver your work.

Try to keep in mind your name, and your business brand when you are choosing a logo or style. If you can think of a cool or catchy play on your brand, then now is the time to go to a graphic designer freelancer and have them draw up something for you.

A great photo of yourself looking professional, confident, and happy will go a long way towards making people have a much better connection with you as a person.

Developing Your Freelancer Bio

People want to interact with you, and they need to feel as if they are talking to a real person. This can go a long way towards people coming back to you, and feeling as if they have established a professional and personal connection with you both as a freelancer and a person.

A short bio that leads into your About Us page is a good way for people to feel more of a connection with you.

Now You Need to Reinforce Your Brand on Your About Us Page

This is the second most visited page on any website, regardless of what it is offering. This is your chance to tell your story and sell yourself to potential customers. You want to not only tell your story, but you also want to sell yourself and sell your services to potential clients. Let them know what you do, and how you can help them solve their problems.

If you are not a writer, use your Freelancer account to find a freelancer to help you write your website content for you. This can also be a useful way to get to know the freelance sites that you are working on. Establishing relationships with other freelancers can also lead towards collaboration or recommendations for future work. They might need your services and recommend you to their clients, and vice versa.

Tell Your Story with Your Online Resume

This step isn't compulsory, but if you feel as if you need to include it, or you have a highly impressive work history, then you may want to include it. Remember, though, resumes can be extremely dry reading, even in some cases verging on plain boring, so make sure that you keep it as light as possible.

Stick to the great work that you have done, and include pictures and visual displays or examples of your work. Don't list every job you have done. Consider this resume as a highlight reel of only the great work you have done.

Add Helpful and Interesting Content to Your Website Through Your Blog

This can be a great way to draw people into your website and keep them coming back. If they are interested in what you are posting in your blog, then they will the need to check back in. This will keep you right in their perspective view when it comes to hiring a freelancer.

Even if you're not a writer, this is another great opportunity to get involved with other freelancers and build relationships. Consider swapping services with someone. If you build websites, and they write, then perhaps you could help each other out and save money.

This is a great opportunity for you and them to cross advertise on each other's sites. Include a small link, advertising who writes your content or builds your website, for example.

Compose a Quick and to the Point Brand Speech

Keep it simple, and let people know how you can help them. Don't have a long list of what you do, how you'll help, and what the results will be. Keep this short and sweet, and you will find yourself converting more leads.

Keep Your Brand Flowing Through Your Social Media Accounts

If you utilize Twitter, Facebook, Pinterest, Tumbler, or any of the other social media platforms, then remember to keep your freelancing brand flowing through all of the same. If someone sees your Tweets, then you want them to be instantly reminded of your website.

Have your website logos and brand logos designed specifically for all of your social media platforms and accounts. Have a professional create your banners, logos, and profile pictures so that they flow well across your entire brand. A few dollars is a wise investment on a quality image or banner, compared to something you try to come up with yourself.

By creating a strong brand presence across every aspect of your freelancing business, it will help people create a link with your brand. Once you have a successful brand, it also opens you up to sell your branding services to other freelancers just starting out in the business.

Good luck with your branding and remember, keep it clear and keep it consistent and the results will soon start to speak for themselves. Build your relationships with other freelancers that will eventually start to lead towards mutual work and shared clients. You never know which client will be the one who opens you up to a long list of future clients and a potential lifetime of opportunities and employment.

Chapter Four: Branching Out and Building Your Own Website

We have covered some aspects of what your website should include and your branding in the previous chapter, so I will try not to cover too much of the same information again.

When you first dive into the online world of freelancing and working, in general, you will come to a point where you feel that you need your own website. If you have never built a website yourself and don't have a lot of knowledge in this area, then the task can look simple, but turn into a nightmare rather quickly.

There are a few different ways that you can approach this:

- *Build your website using a website builder.*
- *Build a website from scratch by yourself.*
- *Pay someone to build your website for you.*

All of these are good and legitimate ways to approach the problem of creating or obtaining your first website. They will all vary in price, from free, to minimal, all the way into quite an expensive venture. It pays to do your research.

Building a Website Using a Website Builder

We will start with building your website using a third party website provider. These following sites will be a good place to start:

- *Blogger*
- *WordPress.com*
- *Tumblr*
- *TypePad*
- *Wix Etc.*

There are hundreds of these sites available online, and they all offer services ranging from free to monthly or yearly plans. There are a lot more sites out there, so I'm not going to list them all as they could fill an entire book! Do your homework, and choose one that offers a plan to suit your needs. Most of these sites offer basic packages for free, but if you want more services, then you will need to pay for premium packages. For the most part, they include hosting and creating a domain name as part of their package.

For someone just getting into working online and creating a website, this could be a quite attractive way to get a basic website at little to no cost. They offer users the ability to drag and drop content and images into selected themes and templates. If it is something more advanced that you are looking for, then you may want to look at building your website.

Building Your Website

If you are Internet savvy already, and consider yourself quite capable of learning some basic website building skills, then you may want to consider building your website. You'll need to purchase a domain name and URL and organize hosting yourself, but this is a relatively simple thing to accomplish, and depending on what you choose can be quite inexpensive. Do your homework and shop around when you are looking at hosting options. Look at their speed of hosting offered, and the support service that the company offers. Check online for any reviews of the company, and compare it to the opposition. Research with anything you do online is a crucial part of any project. A little bit of time researching can save you a lot of money down the road, and also a lot of headaches.

This is where we discussed choosing your name in the previous chapter about branding. When you have your name chosen, then you can look at purchasing it, and getting ready to start working on building your website. WordPress.org, not to be confused with WordPress.com, is a simple and easy way to start building your website. It allows you to choose from thousands of themes, and also to create and edit your own. It may seem complicated at first, but they offer you a lot of support, and there are a lot of tutorials available online to help.

If you need help with website content, images, or graphics, you can choose to go back to your freelancing sites and hire freelancers to help you. They can come up with the different parts of your website that you are struggling with.

This is only a quick guide on the key points; I could write an entire book on how to build a website. There are many different things that you will need to tweak and change as you go along, but by this point, you should have a basic website with some content and images.

At this point, you will be more confident with your site and starting to look into things like SEO and the way the site functions. You can back up your site as you work on it, and then restore it to previous versions if things go horribly wrong. Going online to find the answer to any really difficult problems that you may encounter is a quick and cheap way to fix anything that comes up.

No matter how many websites you build, you'll always end up with small problems or the need to learn something new. The more you work on your website, the easier it will become and the quicker you will get at it.

Paying Someone to Build Your Website For You

If you have no interest, time, or skill for building your website, then you can choose to have one built for you. This is where having connections on your freelancing platform can really pay off. If you know someone who builds websites, then consider approaching them to work out a mutual exchange of work. If not, then you will need to work out exactly what you are looking for so that you can work with your freelancer or website designer to come up with exactly what you are looking for.

Make sure that you get a quote at the beginning of your project, so you know exactly what sort of price you are expecting to pay. This will help both people to be on the same page, and if something looks like it's costing more or less, you will know what's happening.

Websites can be expensive money pits once you go down the road of building your own. Ask for references or examples of people's work and have a look at the work they have done for yourself. If possible, speak to the website administration so you can learn for yourself how well the freelancer worked out.

Remember to keep in mind everything that you have learned so far about branding, and to keep your brand flowing through the website.

Chapter Five: Communication is Key

One of the most important aspects of any working relationship, whether it is on a freelancing site or in real life, is communication. Successful communication with the people you work with and the clients you work for is an important way to establish an excellent working relationship. Obviously, you don't want to harass people, but keeping people up to date, and letting them know that you have received their message or email is a critical aspect to your business relationship.

When you are working online, you don't have opportunities to develop a relationship the same way that people do when they are dealing with clients face to face. Working on your online communication skills will help you to not only secure more work, but it will also help you to keep those clients coming back time and time again.

There are millions of freelancers online, so any advantage that you can get that puts you ahead of the competition is a good idea.

Always Use Proper Language When Speaking With Potential Clients

When we are communicating with our friends and family, it is easy to fall into the bad habit of using slang or abbreviations. It's never going to be appropriate in a business relationship to use any abbreviations such as *Ty*, *gr8*, *4u*, or *yw* for example. After you have been working with clients for a long period, you may use less formal means of talking, but always try to maintain a strict business relationship. Speaking with freelancers about how they speak to potential clients, I have learned how just using correct grammar and spelling has won them jobs from among dozens of other freelancers, some more qualified.

Replying in a Prompt Manner

Some freelancing sites will evaluate and rate you on how quickly you reply to messages that you receive from prospective clients. It isn't normally every message, just the initial message from a new client. Fiverr, for example, has your response time displayed on your profile when potential clients browse your profile. If your average response time is less than a few hours, it could lead to new clients. Many people would much rather engage with someone they expect to answer them within several hours, instead of several days or a week.

You have to be realistic. You are not always going to be able to answer every new message within seconds, but even if you're busy, it isn't a lot of hard work to simply reply and say thank you for your inquiry, and I'll get back to you as soon as possible.

If you feel like you need more time to give them an accurate quote or answer a question, then let them know that. You don't want to rush into committing yourself to something that you either can't deliver or that will end up costing you time and money.

Don't Let Any Communication Get You Frustrated or Flustered

Sometimes, you are trying to deal with someone who may have a different first language than you, or are just plain hard to understand. Just because you think about your responses carefully doesn't always mean that potential clients think about what they want or how they express that. Try not to get frustrated with them, as you never know who is going to turn out to be an extremely beneficial client.

Be clear on how you explain your point of view to them. Don't try and over complicate things if they have a problem with language. If you think it's worth it, try using a video or a screenshot to emphasize your point so that they understand what's going on.

Sometimes, it may be better just to explain to the potential client that you don't have time to undertake their project or that you aren't suited to it. Quite often, if you let people know that you won't be able to the best job possible, they are happy to move on. Sometimes, this is easier than dealing with the result of a miscommunication between you and your client which could end up with you having to either redo work or getting negative feedback.

Always Get Written Confirmation of Any Changes

If you speak over the phone or Skype with your clients or any other verbal communication, it always pays to get everything in writing. This doesn't just apply to changes either, all commitments should be recognized with a written agreement. If you take notes during the call, then you can simply write up a brief report and send it to your client to get confirmation. This is a quick and easy way to get everything out in the open, with no opportunity for any misunderstanding later on.

If You Don't Understand Something, Then Ask

If you have ever dealt with a freelancer or employee who nods and says yes to everything you ask, and then halfway through the project is completely lost or delivers something that is entirely wrong, you'll understand how frustrating it is. There is nothing worse than to not only get something below average, but also something that is not even close to what you expected.

You don't want to be that freelancer; your negative feedback will soon lead towards your rating going down the toilet.

The only way to find out more information is to ask! The best time to ask is before you start a project. This will help you avoid any unpleasant consequences later on into the project. No one is going to be annoyed if you ask a lot of questions at the start of a project, especially if you deliver a great product in the end.

By following these simple steps for successful communicating, you will be that much closer to having a great freelancing career!

Chapter Six: Conclusion and Advice

Well, now that you have all of the essential information that you need to get started on a successful freelancing career, the rest is up to you! Ultimately it pays to do as much as possible to build up your client list and get work flowing into your business before trying to raise your prices. Your client base is the most important asset of your business, and you need to look after it as much as possible. This doesn't mean that you should neglect other aspects of your life or business, but if you have regular clients and want to keep them, then you may need to give them special attention.

Remember that there are millions of freelancers out there offering the same or similar services to you, sometimes at a cheaper price with a better turnaround time. It will be up to you to shine above all of your competition out there.

As a freelancer, you have much more time to spend your time the way you want. Don't fall into this trap, though, just because you put something off one day doesn't mean it will go away! In the end, you will still need to get your work done, and having a relaxing day at the beach could result in a stressful night in front of the computer later. You will need to learn to balance your life and work commitments with your freelancing projects.

Don't be afraid to try to learn new skills. If you can take a course online to learn a new skill, you could open yourself up to new opportunities to make money. This way, you can offer your customers additional services and create new income streams for yourself. Stay up to date with any trends or changes in your chosen field, and you will be on a level playing field with any of the opposition out there.

Make a plan for your business. Work out where you want to be in the future, and how you are planning on getting there. If you feel as if you are falling behind your business plan, then try to get back on track. If you need financial help with your business, the best thing you can do is seek out a qualified accountant. They will be able to make sure that you are following all of your state's or country's tax rules and regulations.

Keep a work diary. Try to keep as far ahead as possible when planning work or quoting clients on new projects. If you anticipate needing longer than normal on an upcoming project, then let your client know. You never want to be scrambling to try and finish work at the last minute; this will only lead to below average quality of work. If your client isn't willing to wait longer, then you will need to accept this. There are only so many hours in a day, and only so much work that you can accomplish without becoming burnt out.

If you need to use programs like Word or Photoshop, then make sure that you always pay for the premium edition. Don't try and get by with free programs, unless it's the only way to get something accomplished. Having the best programs to use will help to increase the finished product of the work, and it will reflect in your quality and the feedback you receive from your clients.

If you have great regular clients, then don't be afraid to give them a discount or reward if you can. This doesn't always have to mean that you give them something for nothing or at a reduced rate, but there are other ways to reward your loyal customers. If they ask for something, then try to get their work done ahead of schedule. If it doesn't affect your other clients, then you can jump their job ahead of your queue.

Remember, if you have built up a relationship with certain clients, don't be afraid to ask for their feedback. If you can start building up a portfolio of work to be displayed on your website with testimonials from clients, it will improve the impression future clients receive when they visit your website. A simple testimonial along with a brief overview of your project can be an excellent tool to display your talents and skills.

Remember to take a break! Get outside and get some fresh air every now and again. Go out for coffee with friends, and enjoy the rewards of your hard work! Stay positive, and keep your spirits up, life is too short to worry about everything, and ultimately it will impact on your health.

Happy freelancing, and good luck on your future of being self-employed and living the dream life, drinking cocktails on a tropical beach while working!

I'm passionate about freelancing and automation, and I'd like to keep in touch with you and send you some more information about working online. If you'd like that information, please click this link: MORE INFORMATION or by going to https://mailchi.mp/1a871d9a8fe3/landingpage

Automation of Your Freelancer Business

As freelancers, it's vital that you spend every second of your day carefully. The aim of freelancing, after all, is to spend more time doing the things that you love and less time working. As a freelancer, it's easy to fall into the trap of working day and night. You see the money rolling in, and everything seems great, but it's easy to lose track of how much time you're spending to make that money.

You need to think about every hour in the day that you spend doing the mundane tasks. What could an extra one or two hours in a day mean for your freelancing business? A lot to some freelancers.

Time is money. It may be an old saying, but it still rings very true! Learning how to control your freelancing business through automation is a great investment in your future earnings. Time is one commodity that you just can't buy. Regardless of how much money you're making through freelancing!

So, how can you make your freelancing business run a little smoother? Automation of your business, that's how! We are lucky enough to live in an age of technological advancement and many of the mundane tasks we need to complete each day through our freelancing business can be quickly and easily automated with a little setup.

Once you have them set up, your automation is complete, and you'll be working smarter and have a lot more time to either get more work done or spend with your family and loved ones.

Many freelancers look at the setup time of automation as restrictive. Creating accounts and templates on new programs can often be quite daunting to new freelancers. You have to look past the setup time and focus on the long-term benefits of automating your freelancing business. Once you have your freelancing business automated, it will often take care of itself and require only minor updates and tweaks in the future.

Don't expect to rush out and invest thousands of dollars automating your freelance business overnight. Automating can be an expensive venture, especially for new freelancers that are just starting out in the business. Take automation one step at a time and focus on free programs until you can afford to upgrade to more expensive platforms. Balance out the expense of automation against the savings. If it's going to cost a lot, but ultimately save you very little, then wait until the costs are more in your favor.

What Could You Automate As A Freelancer?

One of the first things that many freelancers look at automating is their social media. Twitter, Instagram, Pinterest, Facebook, LinkedIn, and many other social media sites can be quickly and easily automated. Instead of logging in and individually posting something five or six times you can create scheduled posts through sites like Buffer. This will quickly and easily allow you to post across multiple platforms and not get sucked into each individual platform.

Many social media platforms allow you to automate within the platforms themselves. This could be as simple as setting up automatic responses to messages. You can give people a lot of information straight away with an automatic reply message on sites such as Facebook Messenger.

Automating Your Email Accounts

It's easy to get sucked into email hell. It's not uncommon for freelancers to run multiple email accounts depending on what sort of work they're doing and often freelancing platforms such as Fiverr, UpWork, etc. all have their own messages and emails.

One of the easiest things that many freelancers do is to keep their emails tidy and organized is to open multiple emails. This may keep them tidy and organized, but now you're having to answer and reply to multiple emails through multiple email accounts.

The first thing that you'll want to do is choose a mail program which allows you to run multiple emails accounts in one location. Now you can open one mail program and have all your emails coming into one place. That's step one in automating your emails.

Step two is to set up folders within your email. All of this may sound simple, but it's the simple things that we often overlook when we start out freelancing. Shoot your emails into the designated folders. Even if you don't reply straight away, this will allow you to focus on important emails first. You can even set up some email accounts up so that certain emails are pre-sorted into their designated folders.

Next, you'll want to set up some automatic replies. If you have contact forms coming from websites, then you can have automatic replies setup to reply with certain designated responses. This will help to filter out people that are just browsing or looking for information.

Now that you have your email accounts set up to take as much of the manual sorting and responding done automatically, it's time to automate your responses — mail programs such as Outlook work in conjunction with other programs like Bells and Whistles. You can create templates of replies. If you find yourself answering similar questions on a regular basis, then create a template for that reply. When someone emails you with a question, drop the template in, and your reply is done in seconds.

Automating Your Schedule

Another thing that may sound obvious but many freelancers overlook is their calendars and schedules. If you have a great schedule set up, you'll quickly discover that you have more time and that you're completing your tasks a lot faster.

It would be great if we could all afford virtual assistants, but for many new freelancers that isn't an option, yet! In the future that could be a solution for you.

If your desk or office is covered in notes and reminders its time to step into the future! One very popular tool for scheduling and reminders is believed it or not Alexa. You can ask Alexa to set you reminders and schedule events. It's quick, easy and doesn't even require you to do any typing.

There are some other calendar tools like YouCanBookMe and Calendly that are great for automation. Both programs allow your clients to simply book time from preset available times. They just pick a time and book it on your calendar. No back and forth and no emails to waste your time.

Managing Your Time

The last thing that you want to do is spend more of your time tracking hours for clients and projects. Another aspect of this is then tracking those hours and turning them into billable hours for your clients and accounts.

There are a variety of different time tracking tools that will calculate the number of hours you have spent on projects, create invoices and send them directly to your client. Invoices are then accounted for in your accounting program, and there's not a lot more work for you to do.

Your clients are also going to appreciate the accuracy of your timekeeping, your accounts and the timely manner in which you bill them. When the end of the financial year comes around, it's also going to be a lot easier to balance all your accounts.

This is also a great way to keep records for future projects which may arise. You can quickly check back on similar projects, work out how long they took you and then quote them for future clients. If projects took longer than expected, you'd be able to identify where you took too long and ways that you can fast track or expedite different aspects of the project for future jobs.

Allow Your Clients To Order Directly

One of the great things about freelancing sites such as Fiver is that it allows the seller to create a gig that the buyer can buy directly with very little interaction. First, it eliminates the back and forth of emails and messages. Organizing quotes and prices for buyers that ultimately go with another freelancer can be very time consuming and frustrating.

Creating set price orders which buyers can order directly without any interaction can be a great way to save a lot of time.

Think of a package which you can sell and then think of prices. Work out packages that will allow you to make money and are easy for buyers to navigate, understand and ultimately purchase. Obviously, packages won't work for every freelancer, but if they work for you, then they can ultimately save you a lot of time.

Managing Your Bills and Accounts

We all have bills and accounts to pay. Creating automation in how you manage and pay all your bills is really easy once you set it up.

Start off creating a budget. Work out how much money is coming in and how much money is going out. Next, work out which bills you need to pay and how much you need to allow for all your bills.

Setup a credit card or account where all your freelancing bills or even personal bills can be drawn out from automatically. If you have $1000 worth of bills each month, then set up your payments, so at least $1000 goes into this account automatically. Now, link this account to your accounting program and track all your business-related expenses.

Now you don't need to worry about bills becoming overdue or accidentally missing an important payment. This is also a massive time saver. You'll be surprised how quickly a few minutes every day paying bills can quickly turn into hours throughout a month.

Project Management Automation

Having a virtual assistant or project manager to manage all your work is the ultimate goal for many freelancers, but out of reach for most new freelancers. You may be surprised to learn that programs such as Trello allow you to manage your own projects easily.

Trello allows you to create a variety of different boards. You can designate different boards for different clients or projects. Then it's just a matter of setting yourself folders within the board to manage specific parts of the project.

You can set goals, checklists, and even percentages as you work through goals. You can share boards with clients, update them on progress and get feedback as you move through the entire project.

You'll quickly fall into the habit of updating and managing your projects as you complete them. If you get to the point where you can afford a virtual assistant or project manager, they'll be able to seamlessly slip into your system and manage your projects for you.

Automation and Freelancing Conclusion

These automation ideas are just some of the fastest and easiest ways to automate your business. You can many of these automation ideas much further in your personal freelancing. How much you automate your business is entirely up to you and the specifics of your freelancing work. Some freelancing business models are much easier to automate than others, so it takes a little bit of time to work out what aspects of your business you can automate, and which parts don't work.

Take your time when you start off with automation. Try and find some free programs to start off automating your freelance business. There are hundreds of different automation programs available; many of them offer either free trials or limited aspects of the program for free. If you find that the program works well and is worth upgrading, then look into the cost of upgrading or try and find a cheaper program that offers you the same benefits.

Often, it takes a lot of time to find the right automation program that works with your freelancing business. Sometimes you'll find programs that offer everything that you need, while others only offer part of what you need.

If an automation process ends up taking you too much time and doesn't seem like it's worth the hard work, then don't spend too long playing around with it. Spend a little time and find the right automation program or process that works for you. Automation can be a very cost effective and time-saving way to boost your freelancing business and take it to the next level!

Like what you've read? I have some SUPERB information I'd like to send you (no spam, I promise!) which you can get simply by clicking this link: MORE INFORMATION or going to https://mailchi.mp/1a871d9a8fe3/landingpage

My Blog

If you would like to stay up to date with any of my great advice, then I would like to invite you to visit my website and follow my blog. This way, you won't miss any critical updates, and I'll be able to pass on some really great information. As I learn new developments, I'll be able to share them with you through my blog.

Here's a link to my YouTube page with more great information on freelancing

https://goo.gl/A6Uf7u

And, if you want to cut to the chase, here's my most popular video on my YouTube page

https://goo.gl/zAA2Pn

Here is a link to my website and my blog

Make Money Working Online

If you would like to visit my author page on Amazon

Robert Kempster Amazon Author Page

Here is my Facebook page, so that we can stay in contact

Robert Kempster Facebook Author Page

And, before you go, here's a little bonus for you who read all the way to the end: https://share.robinhood.com/robertk2982

Sample of "Making Money Online"

If you enjoyed this book, then please feel free to enjoy a sample of my successful book available on Amazon:

Making Money Online: Earn $1,000 to $5,000 Per Month With Less Than $100 Invested

Introduction

If you have a computer and some extra time, you could be earning more money! That money earning potential lies right at your fingertips, with the Internet. All you need are the skills you already possess, and this book.

"Making Money Online: Earn $1,000 to $5,000 with just $100 invested" will provide you with an overview of the many different online jobs available to people with your specific skill sets, and get you started on landing your online dream job with a razor-sharp focus on earning over $1,000 per month.

This book will examine the skill sets necessary to make it in the online job marketplace. In addition, you will preview the many positions available online, and learn how to land those jobs by marketing yourself and your skill sets. This book's chapters will cover not only the basics of some of the most popular web-based freelancing sites, but help you to work through building a strong relationship with your customers by developing healthy online work habits. I must admit that writing it has helped me to reexamine myself, and led to serious improvements. Well over 50 percent improvement in project delivery time across the board.

Online jobs now account for about five percent of the national gross domestic product. Those are dividends that your skill sets can help you capture with minimal investment.

What this book is not: This book is not a - get rich quick – type of book, it is not about affiliate marketing – even though some of the skill set applies, it is not a Guru book, it is not a way to fleece more money out of you, and it is not for advanced readers.

Earning money online has never been easier or more fulfilling for talented professionals. Get started now, and read on!

References

http://mashable.com/2013/06/09/freelancing-getting-started/#F2AZ8cMeDEki

http://www.forbes.com/pictures/mjd45ehhjd/marketing/

https://entwiningwords.wordpress.com/2013/09/22/my-list-of-25-trusted-freelance-job-sites-online/

http://business.tutsplus.com/articles/12-steps-to-building-your-stand-out-freelance-brand--fsw-32044

http://neilpatel.com/2015/07/30/from-0-to-launch-6-steps-to-building-your-first-website/

http://www.dianamarinova.com/5-tips-to-effective-communication-freelance-clients/

http://www.1stwebdesigner.com/25-awesome-tips-successful-freelancer/